Original title:
The Apple Tree's Whisper

Copyright © 2025 Creative Arts Management OÜ
All rights reserved.

Author: Gabriel Kingsley
ISBN HARDBACK: 978-1-80586-381-6
ISBN PAPERBACK: 978-1-80586-853-8

Whispers in the Orchard

In an orchard bright and sunny,
A tree told jokes, sweet and funny.
A squirrel laughed, dropped his snack,
Said, 'I can't hold it! I'm under attack!'

Bumblebees buzzed with a twist of glee,
'No time for honey, come laugh with me!'
The breeze chimed in, a giggle or two,
'If you can't laugh, you might just stew!'

A passing goat, with a jaunty strut,
Heard the tree and called, 'What a nut!'
With every chuckle, the fruits all shook,
Plums rolled down like a playful book.

So if you wander near that place,
Don't miss the grin on that leafy face.
Join the fun, don't miss the spree,
In the orchard, laughter flies free!

Nature's Gentle Confession

In the orchard's vibrant cheer,
Fruits giggle, sharing a secret,
Leaves hold tales of sunlit play,
While shadows dance in breezy ballet.

A squirrel scolds an old gray crow,
Who swipes apples, putting on a show,
But nature laughs and lets it slide,
As worms serenade from deep inside.

Murmurs in the Orchard

Breezes whisper through the greens,
Tickling branches, oh, what scenes!
A bumblebee in a tuxedo flies,
Claiming nectar—what a surprise!

Chickens strut with utmost flair,
Clucking gossip without a care,
While frogs croak tunes of love and woe,
Nature's choir in great show.

Secrets Swaying in Sunlight

Sunlight dapples, laughs in rhyme,
As shadows slip in playful time,
A ladybug in polka dots,
Winks at ants juggling all their pots.

The grasshoppers chirp a silly song,
Confusing a cat who ponders long,
What's this ruckus under the sun?
Nature's jest, oh, isn't it fun?

Blossoms Cradle Hidden Hopes

Petals flutter like giggly girls,
Making wishes with tiny twirls,
While a dandelion dreams of flight,
Painted wishes carried into the night.

A butterfly trips on its bright wings,
Chasing echoes of daffodil sings,
Nature's mischief, a jolly affair,
In every breeze, there's laughter to share.

Remembering Sweet Seasons

Beneath the branches, giggles lay,
Silly memories from yesterday.
With every bite of juicy cheer,
Laughter echoes, crystal clear.

Squirrels plotting on a dare,
Who can climb the highest there?
Chasing shadows, hops and skips,
And candy dreams of fruit-filled trips.

Worms in top hats, dancing tight,
Underneath the moonlit light.
Dandelions serve a feast,
But they forgot the very least.

Seasons shift in playful jest,
With apple cider as our guest.
Funny stories twist and twine,
In this orchard, all's divine.

Hidden in the Shade

Beneath a leafy, sunlit quilt,
Lies a world where joy's built.
Napping birds with dreams so grand,
Strut like royalty, oh so bland.

A raccoon DJ spins at noon,
To the tune of a buzzing balloon.
Squirrels take a break to dance,
While ants hold a parade, by chance.

Joking jackrabbits hop around,
In a laughter-laced, grassy ground.
They've painted smiles on the trees,
Just to tickle the summer breeze.

The shade is where the fun begins,
With pie fights and berry skins.
In secret corners, joy does bloom,
And everyday has an air of zoom.

Conversations in Green

In branches where the laughter sways,
The critters share their cheeky ways.
"Did you hear about the cat?" they tease,
His whiskers tangled in the breeze.

A lazy turtle tells a joke,
It's so slow, it gets a poke!
The hens cluck back with witty replies,
While bees buzz loud, don't be shy!

"Who's the funniest here, you tell?"
"Definitely not that grumpy snail!"
Round and round the whispers go,
As silly antics steal the show.

They plot a prank on Farmer Joe,
With apples tied in a row.
What a sight, a funny scene,
In this garden lush and green!

Whispers of the Orchard Floor

Down below where shadows play,
Silly secrets float away.
A lost shoe and a chubby frog,
Turn into jokes with a cheeky smog.

A mole with glasses reads the news,
To worms and weevils, happy crews.
"Did you hear about the pest?" they jest,
"Those aphids sure don't know the best!"

Crickets chirp with laughter loud,
Joining in the goofy crowd.
The roots and rocks all play along,
In the orchard's quirky song.

When apples drop and giggles burst,
A playful world, it's comedy cursed.
Whispers from the ground arise,
Where humor thrives beneath the skies.

Beneath Canopies of Green

In a forest where giggles bloom,
Squirrels debate what to consume.
A raccoon suggests a nutty snack,
While a bird laughs, 'You've lost your knack!'

Under branches, shadows play,
Trees befriend the bold bouquet.
Bees buzz jokes that lift the day,
Nature's comedy in full display.

Luminescence at Dusk

Fireflies waltz with a wink and cheer,
While crickets croak in tones quite clear.
A frog jumps in to steal the show,
'Don't leap too high!' the owl shouts, 'Whoa!'

Stars wake up with a sleepy grin,
As moonbeams giggle, let the fun begin.
Nighttime antics tuck us in,
Crickets keep the laughter thin.

A Hush Among the Foliage

In the shade where secrets weave,
Caterpillars plot, they won't believe!
A grasshopper springs with a mighty laugh,
'Join my leap; we'll take a photograph!'

Leaves are laughing, fresh and bold,
Spinach has stories waiting to be told.
Roots chuckle as they dig down deep,
Whispered jokes for the daffodils to keep.

The Dance of Shadows

In twilight's glow, shadows sway,
Mice on stilts prance, claiming the day.
A tangle of vines starts a parade,
With laughter echoing under the shade.

Balloons made of leaves float high and free,
While ants dress up in their finest spree.
A snail slips in with glitter galore,
Chasing the fireflies, who beg for more!

Swaying with Solitude

In the breeze, a giggle sways,
Leaves dance funny on sunny days,
Branches bend, they make a fuss,
Who knew trees could laugh like us?

Fruits drop down with a playful thud,
A squirrel leaps in a fruity flood,
He steals a snack with a cheeky grin,
Nature's jest, let the laughter begin!

The shadows sashay in the warm light,
Tickling arms, a jovial sight,
Roots chuckle beneath the ground,
In this silliness, joy is found!

Memories on a Branch

Once there was a worm with flair,
Who wore a hat made of thin air,
Perched up high, he told a joke,
To the birds that laughed 'til they broke!

An ant tried to dance with grace,
But tripped and fell, oh what a face!
The branches shook, the apples grinned,
Every critter knew the fun would never end!

A grasshopper joined in the play,
Singing loudly, come what may,
The laughter rippled through the leaves,
As memories danced in the evening eaves!

Tales in the Twilight

As twilight neared, the shadows stretched,
A doe told tales that quite fetched,
Of mischief done by a pesky crow,
Who wore a hat made of mistletoe!

Squirrels gathered to hear the wise,
With ears perked up and wide-opened eyes,
"Did you see that tumble and twist?"
They chuckled at tales that couldn't be missed!

Beneath the stars, they shared a grin,
With every story, a new laugh begins,
Nature's comedy, a twisty, fun ride,
In the evening glow, where joy can't hide!

Shadows and Sweetness

Underneath the shady bough,
A bee danced round, an odd little vow,
"I'll tickle you with honeyed bliss!"
But oh, the fruit flies swarmed to kiss!

The worms could hear the gossip fly,
"Who wore that hat? Oh my, oh my!"
With every rustle, whispers spread,
As laughter bounced and merry mischief bred!

With shadows stretching, giggles soared,
Nature's playground, never bored,
A festival of fun, a grand spree,
In the orchard's embrace, wild and free!

Dreams of Sunlit Dapple

In a garden where giggles grow,
A fruit with a smile, oh what a show.
The little birds tease, they chirp and sing,
While squirrels dance round, causing a swing.

A shadow of laughter, a bubble of glee,
The sun tickles leaves, a spectacle to see.
With each little bounce, the apples take flight,
They tumble and giggle, what a silly sight!

With juice on their cheeks, the kids will proclaim,
"This fruit's got a joke, it's playing a game!"
Laughter erupts as they munch and they munch,
Each bite brings a chuckle, oh what a brunch!

So here in this haven, where joy intertwines,
The apples are jesters, and laughter like vines.
In sunlit delight, let the fun never cease,
For in every bite lies a slice of sweet peace.

Resounding in the Roots

Beneath the earth, a tickle and tease,
The roots are all laughing, oh, don't you see?
They wiggle and giggle, a joyous parade,
While wriggly worms join, not one is afraid.

Above, the branches sway in a whirl,
The wind tells a joke that makes all leaves twirl.
The bark cracks a grin, it's quite the display,
As acorns join in for a comical play.

The apples pipe up with a cheeky delight,
"Let's roll down the hill, oh, what a flight!"
They bounce off the ground, a jolly old crew,
While giggling out loud, they shout, "Coming through!"

In this rooty realm where the funny is found,
Nature hums sweet tones, a whimsical sound.
So let's raise a toast to this merry old land,
For laughter is best when it's shared, hand in hand.

A Symphony of Sunlight

In a sunny orchard where chuckles reside,
The fruits are all jamming, side by side.
With rhythmic plops, they fall from their perch,
Each landing a laugh, a joyful research.

A symphony plays, the apples take stage,
With melodies mixed, they dance off the page.
"Let's wobble and bop, and twirl in delight,
A giggle-filled concert, good vibes taking flight!"

The bees buzzing by, playing tambourine,
Comedic and clumsy, they can't help but preen.
While butterflies flutter, they join in the tune,
With loops and with scoots, they dance 'neath the moon.

So gather ye friends in this sunny expanse,
Where laughter and music invite you to dance.
For in each little note, a tickle takes hold,
In the symphony bright, let the fun unfold.

Time's Tender Ritual

The clock hits a giggle, it's time for the fun,
As apples announce, "Get ready, let's run!"
They race through the orchard, bouncing with glee,
While shadows of laughter sway on each tree.

A ritual of chuckles, so sweet and so bright,
As sunshine tickles, they prance in delight.
"Don't forget to hop!" yells the elder of fruit,
With a skip and a laugh, they stomp in pursuit.

The sun dips low, it's crunch time for cheer,
With each apple bite, the world disappears.
Time's got a rhythm where fun never dies,
In the midst of the laughter, the spirit just flies.

So cherish each moment, let joy take its course,
For time's tender ritual is laughter's true source.
In harmony sweet, may we always stay free,
In the heart of the orchard, as happy as can be.

Beneath a Canopy of Color

Beneath the boughs all dressed in hue,
The squirrels plot, a mischief crew.
With acorns tossed and giggles loud,
They soon become the craziest crowd.

The apples blush with cheeky glee,
As birds debate, from branch to spree.
Tickling leaves that dance in jest,
Who knew nature could be so blessed?

A hedgehog rolls right down the lane,
Chasing dreams without a chain.
Colors clash in a vibrant show,
As laughter crowds the orchard's flow.

Under sun's bright, playful stare,
The trees ensure there's joy to share.
The whispers of amusing tales,
Bring smiles where the laughter sails.

Threads of Light in Branching Murmurs

In golden sunbeams weaving through,
Wisps of laughter nod and skew.
With shadows that prance and twirl about,
Even the breeze can shout out loud!

A chatty robin sings a quirk,
While ants decide to do their work.
But who can resist a jolly prank?
When bees buzz in a joyful flank!

Ripe fruits dangle like dangly toys,
The gnomes beneath giggle with joy.
They trade their hats for a slice of pie,
And wave to clouds drifting by the sky.

Threads of light chase through the leaves,
While nature chuckles, it achieves.
In every nook, a tale unfurls,
As life dances, skipping twirls.

Reverie in Orchard Shadows

In shadows where the giggles rise,
The wind plays tricks as time flies by.
A family of rabbits, quick on their feet,
Organizes races where they compete.

The shadows stretch, their fingers tease,
While butterflies waltz in the hot summer breeze.
A hedgehog offers to be the judge,
As laughter bounces in a light-heartedudge.

Each apple glows with a secret grin,
Whispers of pranks that soon begin.
With shadows bold, they spin and play,
In the orchard's realm, joy leads the way.

The sun sets low, the day will end,
But sweet camaraderie will not bend.
As night falls, the hum of delight,
Wraps the orchard in soft twilight.

Secrets Hidden Amongst the Leaves

Among leafy secrets, a giggle peeks,
While ants wear capes, oh so unique.
The crickets leap with a rousing cheer,
Sharing whispers that all can hear.

A playful wind tickles the scene,
While flowers dance, bright and keen.
The spots of sunshine, such a delight,
As shadows throw confetti of light!

In the branches, squirrels hold a party,
An invitation to all, so hearty.
With nuts and fruits for a fancy feast,
They declare laughter's never ceased!

Secrets that flutter in every breeze,
Unfolding stories with perfect ease.
Amongst the leaves, joy intertwines,
As the day ends, and laughter shines.

Echoes of the Orchard

In the orchard, apples grin,
Chasing squirrels, let the fun begin.
A fruit falls down, it starts to roll,
Bouncing past the distant mole.

Bees in bowties buzz and dart,
Trying to win the dance of art.
While shadows play on grassy ground,
Laughter echoes all around.

Hats on heads, the critters cheer,
Celebrating autumn's sneer.
A giggling breeze spins leaves so bright,
Under the sunlight's playful light.

Murmurs of Blossoms

Blossoms whisper silly tales,
Of muddy boots and funny gales.
Around the trunk, a raccoon pranced,
Chasing butterflies as they danced.

"Why did the worm cross the path?"
To find some shade, oh what a laugh!
With giggles floating through the air,
The flowers sway without a care.

A duck in shades, what a strange sight,
Takes a dive, with pure delight.
The blooms all chuckle, pink and white,
As shadows stretch at the end of light.

Silent Conversations

Mice in turtlenecks, very neat,
Heavy debates on scampering feet.
With apple cores as their debate,
Quibbles loud, a funny fate.

The wind can't help but crack a smile,
As crickets chirp and joke a while.
"Tell me, why do apples hide?"
"Because they're fruity, and full of pride!"

Twirling leaves join in the talk,
And gossip spreads along the flock.
Underneath the twirls and spins,
The orchard grins at all the wins.

Songs of the Generations

Old branches hum a jolly tune,
While younger sprouts sway, like balloons.
"Remember when the wind was strong?"
"It made the apples roll along!"

Grandma tree, with wisdom wide,
Shares tales of youth with stars as guide.
As laughter lingers in the breeze,
The branches dance with charming ease.

A fruit and nut, both on a date,
Complaining of how love can wait.
The orchard sings, both wise and sweet,
A melody that can't be beat.

Soft Serenade of the Harvest Season

In the orchard, giggles rise,
As apples plot their sweet surprise.
They roll around on the ground below,
Playing hide and seek at a steady flow.

With cada bite, a crunch that sings,
The fruit reveals its playful flings.
Juices dribble, oh what a mess,
A sticky truth, but who would guess?

Bugs do the waltz on a sunlit scene,
Dancing 'round with a jellybean.
Nature chuckles in a leafy sway,
As laughter drips from day to day.

So let's toast to fruit, so round and bright,
Let's dance under the moon tonight.
A harvest of giggles, come join the spree,
In the orchard's laughter, wild and free.

Whims of the Wind-Kissed Orchard

Swaying branches tell a tale,
Of winds that whisk apples without fail.
A cider party had to start,
With all the fruits playing their part.

When gusts arrive, fruits take flight,
Bouncing high, oh what a sight!
One lands on my neighbor's hat,
Guessing he's the new fruit brat!

A bee flies by, doing a jig,
Inviting all for a mushy gig.
While critters grab snacks on their run,
Join the fun, let's make this pun!

So dance and laugh, don't be shy,
In this orchard, we'll always fly.
With every fruit and wind we greet,
The orchard blooms with laughter, sweet.

Enchanted Words Beneath the Canopy

Under boughs, secrets spin,
Apples giggle, inviting friends in.
With chatter and rustle, the gossip grows,
As squirrels joke about winter woes.

A mischievous breeze steals a snack,
Rolling apples down the track.
Whispers giggle, teasing the tree,
While jolly deer give a playful spree.

In clumsy dance, the fruit takes flight,
Landing softly in sheer delight.
With every splash of color, it seems,
Nature beckons us to dream in beams.

So gather close, share a jest,
In this hidden haven, we're truly blessed.
The canopy hums with joy and cheer,
Join the laughter; have no fear!

Dreams Weave through Twisting Branches

Twirling paths where dreams collide,
Apples jest, full of pride.
They whisper cheer from leaf to leaf,
While I chase shadows, beyond belief.

Each step I take, they plop and roll,
Bouncing traits from the tree's soul.
What a sight, to see them play,
In their whimsies, day to day.

Crickets chirp with a syncopated beat,
As ants compete for their tasty treat.
Nature's funhouse, a wacky fair,
Full of surprises lurking everywhere.

So we'll frolic in the dappled light,
Where laughter floats, oh what a delight!
In this orchard of dreams and cheer,
We celebrate every fruity year.

Whispered Blessings of the Orchard

In the orchard full of glee,
A squirrel sneezed up in a tree.
The apples giggled with delight,
As they prepared for a grand flight.

A crow perched high with flair,
Wore a hat made out of pear.
With a wink to the bees in the bloom,
He promised them a dance in the room.

The wind brought jokes that swayed,
Even the branches laughed and played.
Windchimes heard each funny quirk,
Joined in on this joyous work.

So come and taste the sweet delight,
Where laughter grows with every bite.
In every crunch, there's a tale to tell,
Of furry friends where all is well.

Fragrance of Forgotten Memories

Amidst the blooms of scents divine,
A hedgehog danced along the vine.
He wore a crown made of fine thyme,
And sang a tune to pass the time.

Beneath the boughs an old cat lay,
Dreaming of fish, oh what a day!
He twirled in dreams of creamy pies,
While apples plotted sweet surprise.

A bumblebee with shades so cool,
Declared the orchard his own school.
He taught the ants to do the twist,
While trees above couldn't resist.

Each laugh resounds within the breeze,
Echoes of jokes spun with such ease.
In every scent, a memory's born,
In this orchard, never forlorn.

Symphony of Fruiting Moments

In orchards bright where laughter rings,
A turkey danced in golden things.
He sported feathers made of pies,
And hummed the tune of apple sighs.

An owl with glasses on his beak,
Said, "Don't worry, I won't peek."
He laughed as he read the fruity lore,
Creating tales that we adore.

Peaches in a choir sang aloud,
To entertain the passing crowd.
Their notes were sweet like honeyed fun,
While apples jived beneath the sun.

The corn joined in with swaying moves,
As laughter spread, the joy it proves.
In every leaf, a dance, a cheer,
For fruity moments we hold dear.

Divine Presence Between the Leaves

In a leafy realm of fun and play,
A fox cracked jokes throughout the day.
With every pun, the daisies swayed,
As laughter blossomed, never delayed.

Underneath a bough sat a wise old frog,
Reciting poems while smiling like a log.
"Life's like fruit, sweet and absurd,"
He croaked, as the garden heard.

A rabbit hopped with absurd style,
Wore sunglasses and flashed a smile.
He challenged the sun to a race,
While apples rolled about in grace.

Each breeze carried a chuckle clear,
In every nook, there's fun to cheer.
Among the leaves, joy grows and thrives,
In this vibrant place, all humor survives.

In the Heart of Nature's Calm

In the heart of woods so bright,
A squirrel danced in pure delight,
He juggled nuts with flair and style,
While birds just chirped and watched awhile.

The sunbeams peeked through leaves so green,
Nature laughed, a lively scene,
A rabbit hopped with goofy grace,
Chasing shadows, lost in space.

Beneath the sky, a gentle breeze,
Told jokes to all the buzzing bees,
Around the pond, frogs sang their tune,
While turtles smiled beneath the moon.

A dance-off happened near the stream,
With critters bursting at the seam,
The laughter rang, so bright, so free,
In the heart of nature's spree.

Silent Cradle of the Grove

In the cradle where silence sleeps,
A hedgehog took his nighttime leaps,
He stumbled on a sleeping cat,
Who twitched and muttered, 'What was that?'

The owls hooted, full of sass,
As raccoons pranced and made a pass,
In moonlit chaos, hoot and pounce,
A game of tag, they'd all denounce.

Under stars, the crickets played,
With every note, the night conveyed,
A symphony both sweet and mad,
As fireflies blinked, the night was rad.

The trees giggled from side to side,
At woodland antics, wild and wide,
In the grove's hushed, funny embrace,
Nature's jesters hold their place.

Lyrical Secrets in the Orchard

In the orchard ripe and grand,
A goat declared, 'I'm in demand!'
He climbed the fence, a ragged show,
Pretending he was far below.

Apples dropped with thuds and plops,
As squirrels plotted sneaky hops,
They stole a snack, then struck a pose,
While bees bee-bopped beneath the rose.

The farmer sighed, a grin so wide,
As fruit flew past him with great pride,
A dance of chaos in the sun,
Nature's laughter just begun.

With every bite, a giggle grew,
In this sweet land, where joy just flew,
Secrets shared in each crisp bite,
Lyrical tales of pure delight.

Notes of Growth and Rest

In the glow of morning light,
The flowers stretched, what a sight,
They yawned and danced, all in a row,
While bugs played hide and seek below.

The trees stood tall, their branches swayed,
And whispered, 'A little fun is made!'
With twirls and dips, a leafy waltz,
Nature's tune, without a fault.

A lazy cow in sun's embrace,
Dreamed of grass in second place,
While birds dipped low to steal a treat,
The acts of mischief, oh so sweet.

At day's end, with laughter blessed,
Nature sighed and settled to rest,
In textiles of growth, both bright and bold,
Jokes and warmth across the fold.

Vibrations of Verdant Life

In the garden, a sneaky sprite,
Hides behind leaves, full of delight.
Whispers to apples, "Let's have a race!"
They giggle and bounce, oh, what a chase!

Bees wear goggles, buzzing away,
Gathering nectar, they dance and sway.
A squirrel in shades, takes a cool dip,
In puddles of juice, he takes a sip!

A worm in a bowtie, dons full attire,
Sings to the fruits by the old bonfire.
"We're all in this salad, a merry crew!"
They chuckle and cheer, "We'll dress up too!"

The moon peeks in, like a shy friend,
Capturing laughter that'll never end.
With whispers of joy, beneath the bright glow,
Nature's a party, come join the show!

Poetry of Ripe Moments

A pear cracks jokes, oh what a tease,
While young melons sway in the breeze.
The pumpkin grins, quite round and stout,
"Don't be so cheesy," he jokes about!

Ripe strawberries blush, with laughter loud,
As cherries declare they're feeling proud.
They whip up a feast, with fruits on parade,
"Let's show the world how fun is made!"

Bananas are dancing, in bright yellow hue,
Strutting their stuff, doing the twist too.
Lemons toss in, "Let's make it a spree!"
With zesty giggles, they sing with glee!

On a branch above, a parrot calls down,
"Dare you all to paint this fruit town!"
With colors so bright, they craft a delight,
Jokes float in air, till the stars peek bright!

Silhouettes at Sundown

In the dusk's glow, shadows play tricks,
A cucumber sneaks in, pulling off licks.
Tomatoes roll laughing, under the tree,
"Come dance with us, join the jubilee!"

Nightfall arrives with giggles galore,
As carrots reveal they can dance on the floor.
A pumpkin spins tales of the day gone by,
"Adventures in gardens make time fly high!"

Chill in the air, but spirits are warm,
An eggplant in pajamas loves to perform.
The radish takes bets on who'll take the crown,
While laughter erupts, rolling through town!

With winks and smiles, they all hit the hay,
In the warmth of the night, they've had their say.
Tomorrow holds promise, more fun to be found,
As nature's own circus twirls round and round!

The Canvas of Nature's Heart

A canvas spreads under skies so wide,
As nature giggles, brushes by its side.
Colors collide in a vivid parade,
Where fruitful artists craft joy unafraid.

The grapes roll laughter, round and spry,
Painting their portraits, oh my, oh my!
With starlit paint and moonbeam hues,
They craft a collage, of laughter and views.

The wind hums tunes, soft notes in the trees,
While fireflies blink, in a magical breeze.
With brushes in hand, leaves start to sway,
Creating a mural that brightens the day!

When the night falls, laughter takes flight,
As the canvas glows, soft and bright.
In the heart of nature, all critters convene,
To celebrate joy, in a whimsical scene!

The Chorus of Shimmering Leaves

In the breeze, they giggle, swaying low,
Bright green hats, waving to and fro.
"Catch me if you can!" one tree leaf calls,
While the others tumble like a game of brawls.

Squirrels leap like acrobats with flair,
Doing flips while we stop and stare.
The sunbeams dance on a whimsy spree,
Tickling bark, oh so merrily!

Crickets chirp in syncopated beats,
While ants march forward on tiny feats.
Each rustle from above gives a hearty laugh,
As the branches tell tales of nature's craft.

Pinecones giggle, they roll downhill,
Chasing shadows with sparkles of thrill.
A parade of colors, they twirl around,
In the orchard's stage, where joy abounds!

Shadows Speak in Sugary Hues

Beneath the boughs where shadows take flight,
Jellybeans scatter, oh what a sight!
Grapes in the rafters play peek-a-boo,
Oranges bounce like they're in a zoo.

Cinnamon breezes whisper silly rhymes,
While candy-wrapped dreams dance in times.
The sun winks down, a cheeky delight,
As gumball clouds puff in pure blight.

The babbling brook hums a sugary tune,
While mushrooms join in, a funny cartoon.
Lollipops sway, they want to play too,
As rainbows hop like they just flew.

Mirthful shadows leap from branch to branch,
In this orchard, they all love to prance.
With every gust, laughter echoes near,
As whispers of sweetness tickle the ear.

Whispers of Ripened Resilience

In autumn's sun, the apples stand proud,
Winking secrets to an eager crowd.
"Pick me, pick me!" they shout with flair,
As bees in bow ties twirl in the air.

Underneath their rosy-cheeked grins,
Comedic squirrels plot their wins.
They steal a bite, then scamper away,
Chasing shadows till the end of the day.

Pumpkins chuckle, round and bright,
As whispers swirl in the golden light.
"Don't be shy, try a slice of pie!"
As giggly starlings flutter in the sky.

Brittle leaves crinkle, a laugh on the ground,
While hearty laughter lifts all around.
What resilience it takes to bear the jest,
In this orchard, they all feel blessed!

Echoes of Autumn's Embrace

When leaves fall down, they dance and sing,
Flaunting colors like a shiny king.
Beneath the branches, a scuffle and chase,
As critters dash through nature's embrace.

Pumpkin heads bobble, full of cheer,
"It's apple-picking time! Come here, come here!"
With giggles and snorts from deep in the glade,
Whimsical whispers where fun is laid.

The cool autumn air has a spirit so spry,
While candy corn clouds go floating by.
With every swish, the laughter takes wing,
As the orchard bursts forth in a jubilant spring!

So gather your friends, in this leafy dance,
Where silly antics invite a chance.
Echoes of joy, in the crisp, bright air,
In a world where laughter is truly rare.

Fruits of Silent Secrets

In the garden's cheeky sway,
Fruits hang low in bright display,
Giggling leaves in sunlight play,
Secrets shared in light array.

Round and plump, the apples grin,
With a wink, they pull you in,
Their juicy jokes, a sly spin,
A bashful bite where fun begins.

Branches sway, they tease the breeze,
Whispers stir with such great ease,
Laughing fruits, a joyful tease,
Dancing shadows, hearts appease.

Sneaky crows with feathers bright,
Peck on fruits with sheer delight,
Chasing butterflies in flight,
Funny games from morn 'til night.

Beneath the Boughs of Breezes

Underneath the leafy arms,
Mischief brews with all its charms,
Fruits giggle, raising alarms,
Wearing sunshine like sweet balms.

Squirrels slide with acorn hats,
Join the dance, oh how it chats!
Joking vines and chubby rats,
Stealing apples, skilled acrobats.

A parrot squawks, a fruit parade,
While bees hum ballads, never fade,
With every swish, a joke is made,
In this orchard, fun won't trade.

The breeze plays tricks, a playful tease,
Flirting with the warming breeze,
While fruits giggle above the trees,
A merry tune that brings us ease.

Tantalizing Tones of Twilight

In twilight's glow, the fruits conspire,
Bantering sounds that never tire,
With every glance, they teasingly admire,
The laugh of night that takes them higher.

Crickets chirp with rhymes so grand,
While apples roll, a crazy band,
Juicy tales exchanged firsthand,
In this frolicsome wonderland.

Moths flutter by, in curious flight,
Joining in for the evening's delight,
With flavors sweet, they take a bite,
Creating giggles in the night.

Each shade conceals a playful jest,
Ripening fruits, a comic fest,
As stars peep down to be impressed,
By the orchard's master quest.

A Symphony of Ripening Dreams

In orchards where the laughter sings,
Fruits jam out on tiny swings,
With every pluck, the joy it brings,
Twirling colors, make hearts fling.

Mellow pears join in the throng,
Bouncing to a silly song,
Cherries chime, they all belong,
In this fruity world so strong.

From plumpest figs to zesty limes,
Every bite tells jolly rhymes,
With cucumbers that also chimes,
Tales of laughter through the climes.

Even shadows start to dance,
As fruits hold tight their funny stance,
Beneath the moon they find romance,
In whispers sweet, they take their chance.

Choreography of the Wind

A squirrel danced in the gentle sway,
His moves were silly, brightening the day.
Leaves giggled softly, rustling in cheer,
While clouds took note, floating near.

The sun made fun of the dancing trees,
Tickling trunks with a teasing breeze.
Branches giggled as they waved goodbye,
While acorns laughed, "Oh me, oh my!"

Wind's dance partner, the whistling flute,
Brought joy to squirrels, in their cute pursuit.
Together they jived, a fresh new tune,
The whole forest chuckled, under the moon.

Nature's comedy, a show so free,
With gusts of laughter, oh what a spree!
The woods played host to fun-filled fables,
Where every breeze spun whimsical tables.

The Essence of Earth's Care

In the garden, where giggles spring,
Worms wear hats and do their thing.
Roses roll eyes, quite unimpressed,
While daisies chirp, "We're the best!"

Ladybugs sip tea without a worry,
Ants march in, but oh, what a flurry!
Caterpillars laugh, making funny faces,
As butterflies zoom, stealing the traces.

Earth's charm spills over, smiles in the dirt,
Little sprouts tease, it's hard not to flirt.
Gardens are stages, in sunlight they play,
With nature's oddities brightening the way.

Everyone knows it's a jolly affair,
With mushrooms doing a jig in the air.
A scene of oddities, wild and rare,
Nature's own humor, beyond compare.

Messages Carried by the Breeze

A whisper floated, quite absurd,
From buzzing bees, it was quite the word.
"Let's all assemble, let's have some fun!
Today's the day, the games have begun!"

Kites soared high, with mischief in mind,
While grasshoppers chirped, making up rhymes.
Breezes giggled, swirling around,
As butterflies twirled, looking quite sound.

A feathered clown perched on a line,
Singing sweet notes, oh so divine!
While trees tapped their toes, keeping time,
With each rustle, they joined in the rhyme.

Messengers dancing, in glee and delight,
With laughter that carried from morning till night.
The breeze spread smiles, and oh how it flew,
A symphony of joy, all fresh and new.

A Tapestry of Time

Old clocks chuckled, tick-tock through the years,
Woven with stories, laughter, and cheers.
Each second a stitch, threading the past,
A quilt of antics, meant to last.

Sunlight tickled shadows on the ground,
While little ants marched, in circles they found.
A parade of memories, wild and free,
Each moment a part of life's grand spree.

Dust motes danced like comets in air,
With laughter echoing, everywhere!
Time's funny tale, a series of blinks,
With giggles prepared and a sprinkle of winks.

So let us cherish this tapestry bright,
Where time bows down, in the pale moonlight.
With each sunset, a chuckle we earn,
In the garden of moments, the laughter returns.

Shades of Equinox

In springtime's dance, the branches sway,
A squirrel sneezes and hops away.
The blooms all giggle in radiant hues,
As bees play tag with the morning dews.

With winter's chill, the buds shiver,
They trade sweet tales by the river.
A rabbit jumps, a funny sight,
In wooly socks, he hops with fright.

Summer comes, with laughter bright,
An apple fell, a comical flight.
It bounced and rolled, a merry game,
The garden cheered, all called its name.

And autumn's grace, with leaves that whirl,
Spinning around, the trees all twirl.
A breeze comes in, with tickles and grins,
As nature chuckles, and mischief begins.

Love Letters from the Past

Old letters tucked in a tree's embrace,
Love notes scrawled in a hurried race.
A pigeon coos, it finds a rhyme,
As branches sway, lost in time.

With every rustle, secrets dart,
A worm reads poems, straight from the heart.
The wind then giggles, as if to tease,
While squirrels plot their romantic schemes.

The sun peeks in with a teasing gleam,
Two shadows dance like a silly dream.
A couple laugh, beneath the leaves,
Gathering tales of romantic thieves.

Through each season, the letters swirl,
A story told, with every twirl.
From long-lost love, to nature's jest,
In this green world, we find our best.

Harmonies of Seasons' Change

In springtime's chorus, the birds all sing,
A frog in tune, jumps with a fling.
The daisies sway, wearing crowns so grand,
While ants form bands, and join the stand.

Summer's heat brings a show of tricks,
As watermelon drips, and laughter clicks.
A picnic mishap, juice goes astray,
Sticky fingers giggle in dismay.

With autumn's touch, the squirrels engage,
Gathering acorns, they set the stage.
Each leap and bound, a comic routine,
As they prepare for their winter scene.

And winter dawns, with a snowy laugh,
The trees wear hats made of nature's craft.
The snowflakes dance in a silly parade,
While we watch, amazed, in our cozy glade.

A Fortress of Flora

In a garden lush, with colors bright,
Gnomes conspire in the pale moonlight.
They trade their hats, a comical trade,
As flowers giggle, unafraid.

A hedgehog rolls in a ball of spree,
While daisies chant, 'Oh look at me!'
With petals prancing, they put on shows,
As laughter erupts from the roots below.

A fortress built with ivy twine,
A brave young snail on a quest to shine.
A buddy ride on a ladybug's back,
As they explore, they plot their track.

Each bloom a jest, each leaf a song,
In this fortress of laughter, we all belong.
With sunlight streaming and shadows at play,
Nature's humor brightens the day.

A Chorus of Lunar Glow

Under the moon, the apples dance,
A jester's cap, they twirl, enhance.
They giggle in the cool night air,
Telling secrets, none would dare.

A squirrel joins, with acorn in hand,
Planning to steal, oh so grand!
But the apples roll and take a spin,
"Not today, friend! Come join our grin!"

Mice in tuxedos, all lined up tight,
Holding a ball, what a silly sight!
They dip and bow, the grass their floor,
While the apples chuckle, wanting more.

The laughing stars, they wink and gleam,
While dreaming, the apples plot and scheme.
What fun awaits, once dusk does fade?
A fruit fiesta, laughter displayed!

Embrace of the Wandering Breeze

A gust of wind, with mischief to share,
Tickles the apples, tossing their flair.
"Catch us if you can!" they giggle with glee,
As they wobble and sway, wild and free.

The breeze tugs at leaves, a playful tease,
Whispers of joy carry through the trees.
"Dance with us!" they call to the sky,
While nearby critters trod, eyeing the pie.

A robin joins in, singing off-key,
While the apples roll, buzzing with glee.
"You can't catch us! We're delicious and round!"
Laughter erupts, a melody found.

The chatter fills the orchard, bright and loud,
As each plump apple joins the crowd.
And when the sun rises, all will agree,
No fruit is as jolly as those by the tree!

Whispers of Vine's Embrace

Vines twist and twirl, on the ground they creep,
Spilling secrets that tickle and leap.
"Join our cabaret, the fruit chant begins!"
The apples laugh loud, wearing big grins.

The grapes wear hats, with a wobble, not strong,
"We'll juggle with berries! Come sing us a song!"
As the apples nod, they roll with delight,
Chasing the giggles that dance in the night.

A tangle of laughter, the garden's alive,
With a chorus of crunches, the party won't jive.
Bees keep stirring, buzzing their tune,
While the mischievous apples wink at the moon.

But in the end, they share one last joke,
"What do you get when you mix fruit and folk?"
The answer arrives in the soft morning light,
A breakfast of laughter — oh, what a bite!

Echoes of Sweetness at Dusk

As dusk blankets the orchard, whispers arise,
Echoing sweetness under the skies.
The apples convene, oh what a treat,
Swapping stories of the birds on the beat.

"Remember that bee who danced on the pear?"
The others erupt, in giggles they share.
With each tale spun, a sprightly delight,
They sway in the breeze, holding on tight.

The sunset laughs with a tickle of red,
While shadows of night creep softly ahead.
But the apples stay bright, with smiles they beam,
Whispering jokes, a delightful dream.

And just as the stars peek, all aglow,
They bathe in the humor, as laughter will flow.
For in this orchard, with friends all around,
Sweetness is more than just fruit on the ground!

Lullabies of the Leafy Canopy

In the shade, the leaves have tales,
Of squirrels dressed in tiny veils.
They giggle loud, like children play,
As branches twirl in a bright ballet.

The wind joins in with a playful cheer,
Tickling fruits, oh so near!
"Catch me quick!" the bubbles tease,
With laughter shared upon the breeze.

A ladybug plays tag with a bee,
"Who's the fastest? Wait and see!"
The petals dance, spin and swirl,
In this joyous, leafy whirl.

So when you rest beneath the green,
Remember games that've long been seen.
For in this canopy of cheer,
The world's a laugh, come hold it dear.

Fruitful Promises Unraveled

Grapes are gossiping, juicy and round,
"Did you hear? The bananas are drowned!"
Strawberries blush, while peaches pout,
As cherries chuckle, "Let's figure it out!"

The tomatoes laugh, wearing leafy hats,
"Let's start a band with these pillow pets!"
They strum on vines, such a silly sight,
With figs and dates joined in delight.

Lemons spout jokes in zesty tones,
While tiny peas laugh in greeny zones.
"Let's throw a party!" the pumpkins cheer,
As everyone dances, spreading good cheer.

So when fruits gather, know it's no ruse,
They'll share a giggle, no time to lose.
For though they seem sweet and mellow,
In whispers they plot, a fruity hello!

Conversations with the Wind

The wind stirs up all the chatter,
"Mice are playing, oh what a matter!"
With feathers tickling, it breezes by,
While butterflies gasp, giggle, and fly.

"Did you catch that? A joke from a tree!"
The breeze whispers tales, full of glee.
"Thinks it's wise, but it's not at all,
Trying to dance, just waiting to fall!"

Clouds gather, ready for a laugh,
Sharing stories on their soft path.
"Let's rain down some jokes!" one cries,
While sunbeams wink from the blue skies.

So when you feel that playful breeze,
Join in the laughter, if you please.
For nature holds secrets, oh so bold,
In whispers of laughter, forever told.

The Gift of Burgeoning Boughs

Branches sway in a silly dance,
"Let's play hide and seek, take a chance!"
Fruits giggle, swinging, full of zest,
Each branch a joker, wearing its best.

"What's up there?" a birdie coos,
"Maybe a sock or a shoe with hues?"
While acorns tumble, rolling with glee,
As the tree chuckles, "It's just me!"

Leaves poke fun at the lazy bees,
"Wake up now, it's time to tease!"
The breeze and blossoms laugh in delight,
Under the glow of the soft moonlight.

So next time you see a playful tree,
Know it's bursting with giggles, just like me.
For in every bough and rustling sound,
Lies a riddle of laughter to be found.

Songs of Seasons Swaying

When winter's frost wraps all in white,
The squirrels dance, what a silly sight!
They dart and dash with acorns stout,
Planning meals they will talk about.

In springtime's warmth, the buds appear,
Budding romances among the deer.
They twirl and prance around the glade,
In love with shadows that they've made.

Summer's here, the sun shines bright,
The bees are buzzing, oh what a fright!
They're drunk on nectar, each flower's drink,
Stumbling about, they barely think.

As autumn paints in gold and red,
The critters gather, they're well-fed.
With funny hats made from leaves and such,
They dance around; it's all too much!

The Heartbeat of Nature's Abundance.

The wind is giggling 'neath a hat,
While trees sway gently, this and that.
The branches chatter, a playful fuss,
It seems they've had one too many thus.

Little birds brag about their nests,
Claiming their homes are the absolute best.
But a raccoon sneaks and takes a peek,
Declaring, 'This house is just too bleak!'

Lambs waddle forth with clumsy grace,
They tumble and roll all over the place.
Each giggle shared inspires a race,
In the meadow's fun and vibrant space.

Under the stars, the crickets play,
A concert aglow, a wild array.
Nature chuckles at life's grand plan,
As moonlight dances with an ice cream man!

Fruits of Secrets

Beneath the branches, the fruit hangs low,
But whispers of fraud have begun to flow.
"Did you hear the pears are up to tricks?
They've taken the peaches—what a fix!"

The raspberries giggle, their seeds all a-joke,
"Brought in the cherries—a slippery poke!
We'll hold a meeting, no pears allowed,
Just juicy conspiracies, all crowned!"

But then comes the grape with a sly, bright grin,
"Join our grapevining, let the fun begin!"
They all intertwine, with tales to unfold,
Of mischief and laughter and heists gone bold.

Under the moon, the fruits all conspire,
In the orchard's shadows, their laughter will fire.
A banquet of secrets, delectable fare,
Eating and laughing without a care!

Beneath the Boughs

In shady nooks where shadows play,
Rabbits wear hats in a curious way.
One hat is green, with flowers bright,
Another's a mess, what a pitiful sight!

The frogs croak loud, it's karaoke night,
Harmonizing tunes, oh what a fright!
With splashes and jumps, they steal the show,
As crickets applaud, putting on a glow.

A hedgehog disco with moves like the wind,
Spinning and twirling, it's fun without end.
While turtles slow-dance, just taking their time,
Creating a rhythm that's purely sublime.

Beneath the boughs, the moon starts to grin,
Watching the antics that bubble within.
With giggles and joy, the night wraps its arms,
In nature's embrace: a world full of charms!

Embrace of Summers Past

In the shade, we danced and twirled,
With worms and bugs, our friends unfurled.
The fruits above would laugh and giggle,
As we told jokes and did a wiggle.

Sunshine dripped like honey sweet,
We made crowns of leaves to wear on feet.
Each bite of fruit a twist of fate,
Who knew a peach could bruise so great?

Old branches creaked, they joined our play,
"Watch out!" they said, "You're too close, hey!"
We'd swing on limbs, both brave and bold,
While stories of summer would endlessly unfold.

Then came the fall with a sneaky grin,
"Drop on down, let the fruit fights begin!"
We'd toss and babble, oh what a sight,
As laughter rang through the autumn night.

Guardians of the Grove

Beneath a green canopy, we'd hold our ground,
With acorns for helmets, we were glory bound.
Squirrels in armor, like knights of yore,
Deciding the fate of the future's score.

"Protect the fruits!" we'd call out loud,
From sneaky raccoons, oh so proud.
We marched in ranks, our laughter which burst,
Claiming our land, it was just the first.

With sticks as swords, we'd charge in line,
Only to trip on roots—oh so divine!
"Back to the fort!" we'd yell in cheer,
As twigs would crack, it was nothing to fear.

Each battle lost, a victor's feast,
With berries and great big smiles released.
Hand in hand, we'd scale the towers,
Our memories crafted in bloom-filled hours.

Leafy Confessions

Late at night, under the stars,
We whispered secrets, told tales of cars.
Branches swayed while giggling leaves,
Shared stories of tricks and silly thieves.

"Nobody saw me!" said a crow with glee,
"Unless it was that nosy old bee!"
We'd laugh and snack on fruit that fell,
While serenading the breeze with a cheeky spell.

In stealthy shadows, we'd gather round,
Trading old stories, eternal and sound.
Rustling whispers of love's sweet call,
Under this roof, we'd never let fall.

Moonlit confessions, our laughter would rise,
As fireflies joined in, lighting the skies.
The night would end with a sleepy sigh,
And a leaf-loving promise to always comply.

The Language of Leaves

When the wind talks, we listen with glee,
Leaves rustling secrets, as wild as can be.
A giggle from green, a snicker from gold,
Mapping out stories that never grow old.

"I saw a fox dance!" whispered one sprout,
"Right near that pond, without any doubt!"
So we'd huddle close, beneath the sunbeam,
As tales of nature made us all beam.

"Who's that up there? A squirrel on high!"
"Let's throw some nuts and see if he'll fly!"
Laughter echoed through the sunny glen,
As nature wrote stories of silly again.

A language unspoken, with quirks and fun,
In every leaf's flutter, we'd bask in the sun.
Under a sky where giggles take flight,
The joy of our words danced into the night.

Whims of the Seasons

Spring came in bouncing, quite spry,
With flowers in hats, oh my!
Summer arrived with a splash,
Making everyone run, what a dash!

Autumn danced with a mighty swirl,
Gathering nuts for a little girl.
Winter chuckled, bringing in frost,
As everyone slipped, their shoes tossed.

Such pranks do nature like to play,
A comical dance in every way.
Seasons giggle, sharing a tease,
In a world full of vibrant crazies!

So join the laughter, don't be shy,
Watch the seasons wink and pry.
When nature plays, we all can see,
Life's a joke, particularly free!

Breath of an Old Guardian

In the shade of a wise old sage,
Leaves rustle tales of a golden age.
With every gust, secrets unfold,
Of silly critters and adventures bold.

Rabbits giggle as they hop about,
Playing tag while the squirrels shout.
The breeze blares jokes, rich and wide,
Whispering tales of an ancient ride.

From acorn to oak, the laughter flows,
Tickling roots where the funny grows.
Nature chuckles with every breath,
Chasing away the woes of death.

So sit awhile in the green embrace,
And find the humor in this place.
With each gust that tickles your chin,
Join the guardian's carefree grin!

Nature's Lullaby

Crickets chirp in a late night choir,
Bouncing notes 'round the campfire.
Owl hoots softly, a wise old friend,
Singing a tune that will never end.

The brook's a joker, bubbling with glee,
Whispering secrets to the tall pine tree.
Fireflies twinkle, a laugh in the dark,
Dancing with joy, leaving their mark.

Starlight giggles, a twinkle on high,
Winking at dreams that float through the sky.
Nature hums its gentle refrain,
Making sleep come with joy, not pain.

So lie back and let the world snore,
With laughter echoing forevermore.
In this lullaby beneath the moon,
The funny whispers grow all too soon!

Traces of the Morning Dew

Morning stretches with a yawn,
Dew drops shimmer like jewels on the lawn.
Grass giggles, tickled by the light,
As petals wake up, all gleeful and bright.

Bees buzz by with a zesty cheer,
Sipping nectar without any fear.
A sunbeam nudges the butterflies near,
Making them twirl, giggling without a care.

With each drop that falls, there's a splash,
Nature's antics in a joyful clash.
The day is bright, the climate's a clown,
Wearing a smile, don't you frown!

So relish the laughs that morning brings,
With flora and fauna sharing their wings.
Each dewdrop's a giggle, fresh and new,
The world's a stage, and laughter's the view!

Echoes of a Sweet Harvest

In the orchard, apples grin,
Their jokes are sweet and thin.
A squirrel steals a gleeful bite,
Then runs off, his joy takes flight.

Leaves chuckle in the breeze so light,
As fruits plan a funny flight.
One apple drops and starts to roll,
Yelling, "Hey! I've lost control!"

Beneath the tree, kids play and shout,
While the branches dance about.
"Catch it quick!" the laughter flows,
As more apples join the show.

Even the worm has found a friend,
In this crop, the laughs transcend.
With every bite, a giggly smile,
Harvest time is worth the while!

Abode of the Stillness

In a garden where silence looms,
A gnome snores loud as laughter blooms.
His red hat tugs at the wind's soft sigh,
"No peeking! I'm as shy as pie!"

Bees buzz thoughts of honeyed dreams,
As rosy apples share their schemes.
"Hey, did you hear about the pear?"
"What?" "It tried to do a handstand there!"

A ghost of an old leaf flutters near,
"Boo!" it reveals with no sense of fear.
The scarecrow chuckles, planted so still,
"Just wave to him; give him a thrill!"

At twilight's touch, shadows waver and play,
In this stillness, humor finds a way.
Each giggle echoes, soft and bright,
In the calm of a whimsical night.

Mellow Tones of Twilight

When the sun dips low, whispers ignite,
The orchard hums—it's a playful sight.
An apple jests, 'I'm the juiciest of all!'
While the others shout, 'Let's have a brawl!'

Under the moon, shadows toss and spin,
A raccoon sneaks in with a cheeky grin.
"Got snacks for the night? Come and see!"
A shout comes back, "Only if it's free!"

The wind giggles as it flicks the leaves,
As apples plot tricks—oh, what mischief weaves!
A fox peeks in, with laughter he bursts,
"Your fruit salad jokes are just the worst!"

Still, twilight collects these chortles akin,
As the night gathers laughter, rolling in.
With each mellow tone, joy takes flight,
A peaceful symphony in the night.

Fertile Dreams in Bloom

In a field where silly blooms thrive,
The flowers sway, they come alive.
"I'm a rose!" giggles a daisy bright,
"Nonsense! You're just a floral delight!"

A grapevine whispers with a grin,
"Want to guess where my fun begins?"
With grape jokes, hilarity pours,
As twilight arrives, the laughter soars.

A playful breeze tosses hats on heads,
As blossoms waltz and dance their spreads.
"Watch out for wasps with rhythm divine!"
A jest so sweet—it's party time!

In this dreamscape of vibrant hues,
Each petal's joke, a sip of good news.
Fertile ground, where laughter ignites,
Blooming joy under starlit nights.

The Kiss of Autumn

Leaves tumble down, a colorful show,
Squirrels stealing nuts, oh what a row!
The air smells like cider, crisp as can be,
While pumpkins plot mischief, just wait and see!

Kids in their costumes, a wild parade,
Chasing after ghosts, their plans never fade.
Carving big smiles on faces so round,
As laughter echoes, joy knows no bound.

Cider donuts flying, a sugary treat,
While apples are bobbing—quite hard to beat!
Trick or treaters come knocking with glee,
Who knew autumn's touch could be this silly?

So raise your mugs high, give a cheer, my friend,
For fun in the fall is never to end.
Leaves, nuts, and laughter, all in the air,
As autumn dances, with flair everywhere!

Heartbeats Underneath

In the garden where giggles bloom bright,
Worms hold a concert, oh what a sight!
Bees buzzing tunes, with honeyed delight,
As flowers all sway, what a comedic flight.

The groundhogs are plotting, with hats on their heads,
Joking about sunshine and cozy warm beds.
Underneath, earthworms dance to the beat,
While daisies chuckle beneath tiny feet.

The carrots are blushing, all snug in their dirt,
While beans tease the sprouts, "Your leaves look like shirts!"
With veggies in pranks, they twist and they turn,
As laughter erupts, oh how we all yearn!

The garden's a stage, where humor prevails,
With vegetable antics and funny old tales.
So giggle along with this leafy brigade,
For life in the soil is a fun masquerade!

Nature's Quieting Song

In the hush of the woods, crickets start to play,
Whispering secrets at the end of the day.
The owls hoot softly, "Is that a snack, dear?"
While rabbits just grin, "Don't you fret, we're here!"

The brook's gentle giggle makes fish all snicker,
As frogs join the choir, getting quite slicker.
A breeze flutters by with a mischievous tease,
Tickling the leaves, like a playful sneeze.

Mountains chuckle deep, with rocks worn from wear,
Echoes of joy swirl in cozy, sweet air.
Bumblebees buzz ballads, weaving sweet spells,
While nature sings softly, with giggles and bells.

So dance with the shadows, and laugh with the light,
For every soft whisper hides joy in plain sight.
With nature composing, a tune oh so grand,
Life's comedic symphony, across every land!

Wisdom of Wind and Fruit

The wind tells a story with cheeky delight,
Whipping past apples that giggle in sight.
"Catch me if you can!" they dance on the breeze,
While branches bend low, oh please don't sneeze!

The pears are in conference, debating their shape,
"Round is the new style!" they buzz with escape.
Berries are chuckling, "We're tiny but bold!"
As grapes spill their secrets, starting to mold.

The sun offers advice, "Keep growing with glee,"
While shadows keep watching, "Oh let it be free!"
Nature's wise whispers, all playful and bright,
Echo through orchards, a glorious sight.

So laugh with the fruit, let your worries slip,
Join in on the fun, take a sweet juicy trip.
In wisdom of wind, and the fruits' merry plot,
Find joy in the harvest, it's all that you've got!

Nostalgia in the Harvest

In the orchard, bright and grand,
I found a fruit that wouldn't stand.
It rolled away with all its might,
I laughed so hard, what a silly sight!

The branches bent with juicy show,
Bugs danced around, putting on a show.
A squirrel tried to take a bite,
But missed and fell—oh what a fright!

With every crunch, memories cheer,
Of younger days and chums so dear.
An apple pie with a dash of jest,
Reminds us all of nature's best.

Flavor of Time's Passage

Time rolls in, just like the breeze,
With every apple, I feel at ease.
I took a bite, then made a face,
As juice dripped down, oh what a race!

Biting down on this orb divine,
It told a joke from long lost time.
I chuckled loud, it seems so true,
These fruits, they laugh, and so should you!

The sun hung low with a golden ray,
An apple wobbled—'Catch me!' it said play.
I ran to grab that cheeky fruit,
And tripped and tumbled—oh, how cute!

Celebrating the Cycles

Around the tree, we danced with glee,
The apples chuckled, 'Join the spree!'
Each round did toss and tumble low,
We caught our breath with every throw!

The seasons change, the fruits still grin,
'Harvest us!' they coaxed with a spin.
Through twists and turns, we laughed all day,
For every ripened sweet bouquet.

In sunny fields, we raised a cheer,
For every fruit, a joke we share.
An orchard's jest, a vine so stout,
Life's a comedy, without a doubt!

Joys of the Gathering

A basket filled with round delight,
We gathered fruits till late at night.
Each one shared a silly tale,
Of wobbly rides and gusty gales!

The laughter echoed through the trees,
As apples juggled with the breeze.
'Pick me next!' one seemed to shout,
With every fall, there came a rout!

We danced around with cider spills,
A splash of fun among the thrills.
In every bite, a giggle bloomed,
While sweet aromas filled the room!

www.ingramcontent.com/pod-product-compliance
Lightning Source LLC
Chambersburg PA
CBHW062107280426
43661CB00086B/286